FRENCh VOCABULARY BANK

ENGLISH-FRENCH BILINGUAL VOCABULARY BOOK OF ESSENTIAL FRENCH WORDS AND PHRASES

ANCHAL VERMA

Also by Anchal Verma

Littérature Fantastique Belge et Belgitude: Étude des nouvelles fantastiques de Jean Ray

My Weekly French Journal: A Year-52-week Goal Tracking Journal for French learners with French proverbs, French tongue twisters, a list of useful French expressions and plenty of other bonus material

My French Notebook: Ruled 6 sections Notebook/Diary with some useful French expressions

My Language Notebook: Ruled 6 sections Notebook with some useful expressions in different languages

This is my family C'est ma famille: A bilingual English French children's colourful family photo book and beginner book for learning French

For more information about Anchal Verma and her books, visit her website at https://anchalverma.com/

Table des matières
(Table of contents)

Note for learners:

This book is divided thematically and by the end of this book you will know 648 essential words/phrases in English and in French.
Please note that the list of words/phrases in each category (like countries, adjectives etc) is not an exhaustive list (of words/phrases) in that particular category, but includes only the essential words/phrases.

Note pour les apprenants:

Ce livre est divisé de façon thématique et à la fin de ce livre, vous connaîtrez 648 mots/phrases essentiels en anglais et en français.
Veuillez noter que la liste de mots/phrases dans chaque catégorie (comme les pays, les adjectifs, etc) n'est pas une liste exhaustive (de mots/phrases) dans cette catégorie particulière, mais comprend uniquement les mots/ phrases essentiels.

<u>Abréviations utilisées (Abbreviations used)</u>

1. m=masculin (masculine)
2. f= féminin (feminine)
3. s= singulier (singular)
4. pl=pluriel (plural)
5. fr= soutenu (formal)
6. infr= familier (informal)
7. mpl= masculin et pluriel (masculine and plural)
8. fpl= féminin et pluriel (feminine and plural)
9. (m)(f)= masculin et féminin (masculine and feminine)

Salutations et présentations (Greetings and introductions)

S.No.	ENGLISH	FRENCH
1.	Hi	Salut
2.	Hello, Good morning, Good afternoon	Bonjour
3.	Good evening	Bonsoir
4.	Good night	Bonne nuit
5.	Goodbye	Au revoir
6.	How are you?	Ça va? (infr)
7.	How are you?	Comment vas-tu? (infr)
8.	How are you?	Comment allez-vous? (fr)
9.	Fine, thank you	Bien, merci
10.	Not bad	Pas mal
11.	Not well	Pas bien
12.	Ok/so so	Comme ci, comme ça
13.	Good day	Bonne journée!
14.	See you later	À plus tard!
15.	See you tomorrow	À demain!

16.	Nice to meet you	Enchanté (m) Enchantée (f)
17.	What is your name?	Comment tu t'appelles? (infr)
18.	What is your name?	Comment vous appelez-vous? (fr)
19.	What's your name?	Quel est ton nom? (infr) Quel est votre nom? (fr)
20.	What's his name?	Comment il s'appelle?
21.	What's her name?	Comment elle s'appelle?
22.	My name is	Mon prénom est
23.	My last name/surname is	Mon nom de famille est
24.	My name is	Je m'appelle
25.	I am	Je suis
26.	This is	Voici
27.	His name is	Il s'appelle
28.	Her name is	Elle s'appelle

Mots et phrases utiles (Useful words and phrases)

29.	Yes	Oui
30.	No	Non
31.	Okay	D'accord
32.	Mr.	Monsieur
33.	Mrs.	Madame
34.	Miss	Mademoiselle
35.	I	Je
36.	I have	J'ai
37.	You	Tu (infr)
38.	You	Vous (fr) (pl)
39.	I am sorry	Je suis désolé(m) /désolée(f)
40.	Excuse me	Pardon
41.	Thank you	Merci
42.	You are welcome	De rien
43.	Please	S'il te plaît (infr)
44.	Please	S'il vous plaît (fr)
45.	How old are you?	Quel âge avez-vous? (fr)

46.	How old are you?	Quel âge as-tu? (infr)
47.	Where do you live?	Où habitez-vous? (fr)
48.	Where do you live?	Où habites-tu? (infr)
49.	I live in Canada	J'habite au Canada
50.	What is your nationality?	Quelle est votre nationalité? (fr)
51.	What is your nationality?	Quelle est ta nationalité? (infr)
52.	Do you speak French?	Parlez-vous français? (fr)
53.	I don't know	Je ne sais pas
54.	I don't understand	Je ne comprend pas
55.	I love	J'aime
56.	I hate	Je déteste
57.	What is it?	Qu'est-ce que c'est?
58.	I would like	Je voudrais/ J'aimerais
59.	Me too	Moi aussi
60.	And you?	Et toi? (infr) Et vous? (fr)

61.	Nah, its ok	Bof
62.	I am hungry	J'ai faim
63.	I am thirsty	J'ai soif
64.	I am sleepy	J'ai sommeil
65.	Have a good journey!	Bon voyage!
66.	Happy Birthday!	Bon anniversaire!
67.	Happy New Year!	Bonne Année!
68.	I miss you	Tu me manques
69.	I love you	Je t'aime
70.	Good luck!	Bon courage!
71.	There is/there are	Il y a
72.	What a pity!	Quel dommage!
73.	What's up ?	Quoi de neuf ?
74.	My telephone number is	Mon numéro de téléphone est
75.	I dream of	Je rêve de
76.	Listen carefully	Écoutez-bien

J'ai des problèmes... I'm in trouble...

77.	Sorry to bother you	Excusez-moi pour le dérangement
78.	I have a question	J'ai une question
79.	I have a problem	J'ai un problème
80.	Do you speak English?	Parlez-vous anglais?
81.	I speak a little French	Je parle un peu de français
82.	How do you say '…' in French?	Comment dit-on '….' en français?
83.	Excuse me, where is….?	Excusez-moi, où est…?
84.	Please repeat	Répétez, s'il vous plaît
85.	Speak slowly please	Parlez lentement s'il vous plaît
86.	Could you…?	Pourriez-vous…?
87.	One more time	Encore une fois

Temps (Weather)

88.	How's the weather outside?	Il fait quel temps dehors ?
89.	It's hot	Il fait chaud
90.	It's cold	Il fait froid
91.	It's raining	Il pleut
92.	It's snowing	Il neige
93.	It's nice outside	Il fait beau
94.	The weather's bad	Il fait mauvais
95.	It's cool	Il fait frais
96.	It's cloudy	Il fait nuageux
97.	Its sunny	Il y a du soleil
98.	It's stormy	Il fait orageux

<u>Nombres cardinaux (Cardinal numbers)</u>

S.No.	English	French
99.	Zero	Zéro
100.	One	Un
101.	Two	Deux
102.	Three	Trois
103.	Four	Quatre
104.	Five	Cinq
105.	Six	Six
106.	Seven	Sept
107.	Eight	Huit
108.	Nine	Neuf
109.	Ten	Dix
110.	Eleven	Onze
111.	Twelve	Douze
112.	Thirteen	Treize
113.	Fourteen	Quatorze

114.	Fifteen	Quinze
115.	Sixteen	Seize
116.	Seventeen	Dix-sept
117.	Eighteen	Dix-huit
118.	Nineteen	Dix-neuf
119.	Twenty	Vingt
120.	Thirty	Trente
121.	Forty	Quarante
122.	Fifty	Cinquante
123.	Sixty	Soixante
124.	Seventy	Soixante-dix
125.	Eighty	Quatre-vingts
126.	Ninety	Quatre-vingt-dix
127.	One hundred	Cent
128.	One hundred one	Cent un
129.	Two hundred	Deux cents
130.	Five hundred	Cinq cents

131.	Ten thousand	Dix mille
132.	One hundred thousand (One Lakh)	Cent mille
133.	One million	Un million
134.	One billion	Un billion

<u>Nombres ordinaux (Ordinal Numbers)</u>

S.No.	English	French
135.	First	Premier (m) Première (f)
136.	Second	Deuxième
137.	Third	Troisième
138.	Fourth	Quatrième
139.	Fifth	Cinquième
140.	Sixth	Sixième
141.	Seventh	Septième
142.	Eighth	Huitième
143.	Ninth	Neuvième
144.	Tenth	Dixième
145.	Eleventh	Onzième
146.	Twelfth	Douzième
147.	Thirteenth	Treizième
148.	Fourteenth	Quatorzième
149.	Fifteenth	Quinzième

150.	Sixteenth	Seizième
151.	Seventeenth	Dix-septième
152.	Eighteenth	Dix-huitième
153.	Nineteenth	Dix-neuvième
154.	Twentieth	Vingtième
155.	Twenty-first	Vingt et unième
156.	Thirtieth	Trentième
157.	Fortieth	Quarantième
158.	Fiftieth	Cinquantième
159.	Sixtieth	Soixantième
160.	Seventieth	Soixante-dixième
161.	Eightieth	Quatre-vingtième
162.	Ninetieth	Quatre-vingt-dixième
163.	One hundredth	Centième
164.	One thousandth	Millième
165.	Millionth	Millionième

<u>Heure (Time)</u>

166.	What time is it?	Quelle heure est-il?
167.	It's noon	Il est midi
168.	It's midnight	Il est minuit
169.	It's one o'clock	Il est une heure
170.	It's two o'clock	Il est deux heures
171.	Its 2:05	Il est deux heures cinq
172.	It's 2:15	Il est deux heures et quart
173.	It's 3:30	Il est trois heures et demie
174.	It's 4:45	Il est cinq heures moins le quart
175.	It's 7:50	Il est huit heures moins dix
176.	It's 6 a.m.	Il est six heures du matin

Jours et mois (Days and months)

177.	Day	Jour (m)
178.	Week	Semaine (f)
179.	Month	Mois (m)
180.	Year	An (m) Année (f)

Jours de la semaine (Days of the week)

181.	Monday	Lundi
182.	Tuesday	Mardi
183.	Wednesday	Mercredi
184.	Thursday	Jeudi
185.	Friday	Vendredi
186.	Saturday	Samedi
187.	Sunday	Dimanche

Mois de l'année (Months of the year)

188.	January	Janvier
189.	February	Février
190.	March	Mars
191.	April	Avril

192.	May	Mai
193.	June	Juin
194.	July	Juillet
195.	August	Août
196.	September	Septembre
197.	October	Octobre
198.	November	Novembre
199.	December	Décembre

<u>Moments et repas de la journée (Moments and meals of the day)</u>

<u>Moments de la journée (Moments of the day)</u>

200.	Sunrise	Lever du soleil (m)
	Sunset	Coucher du soleil (m)
201.	Morning	Matin (m) Matinée (f)
202.	Midday	Midi (m)
203.	Afternoon	Après-midi (m) (f)
204.	Evening	Soir (m) Soirée (f)
205.	Night	Nuit (f)
206.	Midnight	Minuit (m)

<u>Repas de la journée (Meals of the day)</u>

207.	Breakfast	Petit-déjeuner (m)
208.	Lunch	Déjeuner (m)
209.	Tea	Goûter (m)
210.	Dinner	Dîner (m)

<u>Pays (Countries)</u>

211.	France	France (f)
212.	England	Angleterre (f)
213.	Germany	Allemagne (f)
214.	Belgium	Belgique (f)
215.	Netherlands	Pays-Bas (mpl)
216.	Switzerland	Suisse (f)
217.	India	Inde (f)
218.	Italy	Italie (f)
219.	Canada	Canada (m)
220.	United States	États-Unis (mpl)
221.	Spain	Espagne (f)
222.	Morocco	Maroc (m)
223.	China	Chine (f)
224.	Japan	Japon (m)
225.	Russia	Russie (f)
226.	Nepal	Népal (m)
227.	Malaysia	Malaisie (f)
228.	Singapore	Singapour (f)
229.	Thailand	Thaïlande (f)

230.	Portugal	Portugal (m)
231.	Senegal	Sénégal (m)
232.	Australia	Australie (f)
233.	New Zealand	Nouvelle-Zélande (f)

<u>Nationalités (Nationalities)</u>

234.	English	Anglais (m) Anglaise (f)
235.	American	Américain (m) Américaine (f)
236.	French	Français (m) Française (f)
237.	German	Allemand (m) Allemande (f)
238.	Spanish	Espagnol (m) Espagnole (f)
239.	Italian	Italien (m) Italienne (f)
240.	Indian	Indien (m) Indienne (f)
241.	Canadian	Canadien (m) Canadienne (f)
242.	Japanese	Japonais (m) Japonaise (f)
243.	Chinese	Chinois (m) Chinoise (f)
244.	Swiss	Suisse (m) (f)
245.	Belgian	Belge (m) (f)
246.	Russian	Russe (m) (f)

247.	Australian	Australien (m) Australienne (f)
248.	Portuguese	Portugais (m) Portugaise (f)
249.	Dutch	Néerlandais (m) Néerlandaise (f)
250.	Senegalese	Sénégalais (m) Sénégalaise (f)
251.	New Zealander	Néo-Zélandais (m) Néo-Zélandaise (f)
252.	Moroccan	Marocain (m) Marocaine (f)
253.	Nepalese	Népalais (m) Népalaise (f)
254.	Malaysian	Malaisien (m) Malaisienne (f)
255.	Singaporean	Singapourien (m) Singapourienne (f)
256.	Thai	Thaïlandais (m) Thaïlandaise (f)

Océans et continents (Oceans and continents)

Océans (Oceans)

257.	Atlantic Ocean	Océan Atlantique (m)
258.	Indian Ocean	Océan Indien (m)
259.	Pacific Ocean	Océan Pacifique (m)
260.	Arctic Ocean	Océan Arctique (m)
261.	Antarctic Ocean	Océan Antarctique (m)

Continents (Continents)

262.	Europe	Europe (f)
263.	North America	Amérique du Nord (f)
264.	South America	Amérique du Sud (f)
265.	Africa	Afrique (f)
266.	Asia	Asie (f)
267.	Antarctica	Antarctique (m)
268.	Australia	Australie (f)

Situation familiale (Marital status)

269.	Married	Marié (m) Mariée (f)
270.	Single	Célibataire (m) (f)
271.	Widow	Veuve (f)
272.	Widower	Veuf (m)
273.	Divorced	Divorcé (m) Divorcée (f)
274.	Separated	Séparé (m) Séparée (f)

<u>Professions (Professions)</u>

275.	Student	Étudiant (m) Étudiante (f)
276.	Teacher	Professeur (m) Professeure (f)
277.	Translator	Traducteur (m) Traductrice (f)
278.	Architect	Architecte (m) (f)
279.	Journalist	Journaliste (m) (f)
280.	Writer	Écrivain (m) Écrivaine (f)
281.	Banker	Banquier (m) Banquière (f)
282.	Lawyer	Avocat (m) Avocate (f)
283.	Chartered accountant	Expert-comptable (m) (f)
284.	Engineer	Ingénieur (m) Ingénieure (f)
285.	Actor	Acteur (m) Actrice (f)

286.	Dancer	Danseur (m) Danseuse (f)
287.	Pilot	Pilote (m) (f)
288.	Musician	Musicien (m) Musicienne (f)
289.	Singer	Chanteur (m) Chantrice (f)
290.	Businessman	Homme d'affaires (m)
291.	Homemaker	Femme au foyer (f)
292.	Doctor	Médecin (m) (f)
293.	Nurse	Infirmier (m) Infirmière (f)
294.	Librarian	Bibliothécaire (m) (f)
295.	Plumber	Plombier (m) Plombière (f)

Santé (Health)

296.	I'm sick	Je suis malade
297.	I'm allergic to …	Je suis allergique à ….
298.	Call an ambulance	Appelez une ambulance
299.	I hurt here	J'ai mal ici
300.	I have a headache	J'ai mal à la tête
301.	I have a stomach ache	J'ai mal à l'estomac
302.	I need a doctor	J'ai besoin d'un médecin
303.	I have a toothache	J'ai mal aux dents
304.	I have a sore throat	J'ai mal à la gorge
305.	I have a cold	J'ai un rhume
306.	I'm in pain	Je souffre
307.	I have fever	J'ai de la fièvre

308.	I feel faint	J'ai la tête qui tourne
309.	I'm injured	Je suis blessé (m) /blessée (f)
310.	I had an accident	J'ai eu un accident
311.	Help me	Aidez-moi
312.	I'm diabetic	Je suis diabétique
313.	I have a heart condition	Je suis cardiaque

<u>Famille (Family)</u>

314.	Sister	Sœur (f)
315.	Brother	Frère (m)
316.	Mother	Mère (f)
317.	Father	Père (m)
318.	Parents	Parents (mpl)
319.	Grandmother	Grand-mère (f)
320.	Grandfather	Grand-père (m)
321.	Grandson	Petit-fils (m)
322.	Granddaughter	Petite-fille (f)
323.	Half-brother	Demi-frère (m)
324.	Half-sister	Demi-sœur (f)
325.	Mother-in-law, stepmother	Belle-mère (f)
326.	Father-in-law, stepfather	Beau-père (m)

327.	Sister-in-law, stepsister	Belle-sœur (f)
328.	Brother-in-law, stepbrother	Beau-frère (m)
329.	Son-in-law, stepson	Beau-fils (m)
330.	Daughter-in-law, stepdaughter	Belle-fille (f)
331.	Aunt	Tante (f)
332.	Uncle	Oncle (m)
333.	Cousin (brother)	Cousin (m)
334.	Cousin (sister)	Cousine (f)
335.	Nephew	Neveu (m)
336.	Niece	Nièce (f)

Émotions (Emotions)

337.	Happy	Heureux (m) Heureuse (f)
338.	Unhappy	Malheureux (m) Malheureuse (f)
339.	Pleased	Content (m) Contente (f)
340.	Dissatisfied	Mécontent (m) Mécontente (f)
341.	Nervous	Nerveux (m) Nerveuse (f)
342.	Proud	Fier (m) Fière (f)
343.	Angry	Fâché (m) Fâchée (f)
344.	Indifferent	Indifférent (m) Indifférente (f)
345.	Bored	Ennuyé (m) Ennuyée (f)
346.	Excited	Excité (m) Excitée (f)
347.	Depressed	Déprimé (m) Déprimée (f)

Animaux (Animals)

348.	Dog	Chien (m) Chienne (f)
349.	Cat	Chat (m) Chatte (f)
350.	Rabbit	Lapin (m) Lapine (f)
351.	Cow	Vache (f)
352.	Bull	Taureau (m)
353.	Sheep	Mouton (m)
354.	Goat	Chèvre (f)
355.	Horse	Cheval (m)
356.	Lion Lioness	Lion (m) Lionne (f)
357.	Tiger Tigress	Tigre (m) Tigresse (f)

Lieux (Places)

358.	Cafe	Café (m)
359.	Theatre	Théâtre (m)
360.	Shopping mall	Centre commercial (m)
361.	Church	Église (f)
362.	Temple	Temple (m)
363.	Mosque	Mosquée (f)
364.	Monastery	Monastère (m)
365.	Market	Marché (m)
366.	Restaurant	Restaurant (m)
367.	Movie theatre	Cinéma (m)
368.	Opera house	Opéra (m)

<u>Boissons (Beverages)</u>

369.	Coffee	Café (m)
370.	Tea	Thé (m)
371.	Milk	Lait (m)
372.	Water	Eau (f)
373.	Wine	Vin (m)
374.	Beer	Bière (f)
375.	Soda water	Soda (m)
376.	Milkshake	Lait frappé (m)
377.	Smoothie	Smoothie (m)
378.	Cocktail	Cocktail (m)
379.	Lemonade	Citronnade (f)

<u>Snacks (Snacks)</u>

380.	Sandwich	Sandwich (m)
381.	Fries	Frites (fpl)
382.	Pizza	Pizza (f)
383.	Cake	Gâteau (m)
384.	Chocolate	Chocolat (m)
385.	Bread	Pain (m)
386.	Butter	Beurre (m)
387.	Cheese	Fromage (m)
388.	Soup	Soupe (f)
389.	Doughnut	Beignet (m)
390.	Noodles	Nouilles (fpl)
391.	Tart	Tarte (f)
392.	Ketchup	Ketchup (m)
393.	Hamburger	Hamburger (m)

394.	Steak	Steak (m)
395.	Sausage	Saucisse (f)
396.	Cereal	Céréale (f)

<u>Légumes (Vegetables)</u>

397.	Potato	Pomme de terre (f)
398.	Tomato	Tomate (f)
399.	Carrot	Carotte (f)
400.	Cabbage	Chou (m)
401.	Cauliflower	Chou-fleur (m)
402.	Mushroom	Champignon (m)
403.	Bean	Haricot (m)
404.	Corn	Maïs (m)
405.	Ginger	Gingembre (m)
406.	Garlic	Ail (m)
407.	Capsicum	Poivron (m)

<u>Fruits (Fruits)</u>

408.	Apple	Pomme (f)
409.	Banana	Banane (f)
410.	Grape	Raisin (m)
411.	Cherry	Cerise (f)
412.	Orange	Orange (f)
413.	Pineapple	Ananas (m)
414.	Mango	Mangue (f)
415.	Pear	Poire (f)
416.	Peach	Pêche (f)
417.	Pomegranate	Grenade (f)
418.	Watermelon	Pastèque (f)

Épices (Spices)

419.	Sugar	Sucre (m)
420.	Salt	Sel (m)
421.	Pepper	Poivre (m)
422.	Oregano	Origan (m)
423.	Cinnamon	Cannelle (f)
424.	Coriander	Coriandre (f)
425.	Turmeric	Curcuma (m)
426.	Cumin	Cumin (m)

<u>Couleurs (Colors)</u>

427.	Blue	Bleu (m)
428.	Red	Rouge (m)
429.	Yellow	Jaune (m)
430.	Green	Vert (m)
431.	Black	Noir (m)
432.	Brown	Marron (m)
433.	Orange	Orange (m)
434.	Purple	Violet (m)
435.	Grey	Gris (m)
436.	White	Blanc (m)
437.	Pink	Rose (m)

Adjectifs (Adjectives)

438.	Easy	Facile (m) (f)
439.	Difficult	Difficile (m) (f)
440.	Interesting	Intéressant (m) Intéressante (f)
441.	Handsome	Beau (m)
442.	Beautiful	Belle (f)
443.	Pretty	Joli (m) Jolie (f)
444.	Ugly	Moche (m) (f)
445.	Small	Petit (m) Petite (f)
446.	Tall	Grand (m) Grande (f)
447.	Thin	Mince (m) (f)
448.	Fat	Gros (m) Grosse (f)
449.	Bad	Mauvais (m) Mauvaise (f)
450.	Good	Bon (m) Bonne (f)

451.	Kind	Gentil (m) Gentille (f)
452.	Mean	Méchant (m) Méchante (f)
453.	Polite	Poli (m) Polie (f)
454.	Impolite	Impoli (m) Impolie (f)
455.	Average	Moyen (m) Moyenne (f)
456.	Intelligent	Intelligent (m) Intelligente (f)
457.	Stupid	Stupide (m) (f)

Adverbes (Adverbs)

458.	Today	Aujourd'hui
459.	Yesterday	Hier
460.	Tomorrow	Demain
461.	The day after tomorrow	Après-demain
462.	The day before yesterday	Avant-hier
463.	Very	Très
464.	Also	Aussi
465.	A lot	Beaucoup
466.	A little	Un peu
467.	Not much	Peu
468.	So much	Tant
469.	So many	Tant de
470.	Never	Jamais

471.	Always	Toujours
472.	Sometimes	Quelquefois
473.	Everywhere	Partout
474.	Still, yet	Encore

Prépositions (Prepositions)

475.	For	Pour
476.	Against	Contre
477.	Near	Près de
478.	Far	Loin de
479.	Behind	Derrière
480.	In front of	Devant
481.	During	Pendant
482.	Of, from	De
483.	On top of	Sur
484.	Under	Sous
485.	With	Avec
486.	Without	Sans
487.	In, at, to	À

488.	Except	Sauf
489.	After	Après
490.	Before	Avant
491.	In	Dans

<u>Conjonctions (Conjunctions)</u>

492.	And	Et
493.	Or	Ou
494.	But	Mais
495.	But	Or
496.	Because	Car
497.	So, therefore	Donc
498.	Neither…nor…, Either…or…	Ni
499.	Like	Comme
500.	Since	Puisque
501.	When, as soon as	Lorsque
502.	If	Si

Mots interrogatifs (Interrogative words)

503.	When	Quand
504.	How much	Combien
505.	How many	Combien de
506.	Who	Qui
507.	How	Comment
508.	Why	Pourquoi
509.	Where	Où
510.	Which, what	Quel
511.	What	Quoi
512.	Does, do	Est-ce que
513.	Is, are	Est-ce que

<u>Verbes essentiels (Essential verbs)</u>

514.	To speak	Parler
515.	To love	Aimer
516.	To hate	Détester
517.	To work	Travailler
518.	To listen	Écouter
519.	To come	Venir
520.	To go	Aller
521.	To be	Être
522.	To have	Avoir
523.	To ask	Demander
524.	To write	Écrire
525.	To read	Lire
526.	To say	Dire
527.	To go out	Sortir

528.	To give	Donner
529.	To think	Penser
530.	To watch	Regarder

<u>Parties du corps (Parts of the body)</u>

531.	Head	Tête (f)
532.	Shoulder	Épaule (f)
533.	Back	Dos (m)
534.	Neck	Cou (m)
535.	Chest	Poitrine (f)
536.	Stomach	Ventre (m)
537.	Arm	Bras (m)
538.	Elbow	Coude (m)
539.	Hand	Main (f)
540.	Wrist	Poignet (m)
541.	Finger	Doigt (m)
542.	Hip	Hanche (f)
543.	Leg	Jambe (f)
544.	Knee	Genou (m)
545.	Ankle	Cheville (f)
546.	Foot	Pied (m)
547.	Toe	Orteil (m)

<u>Parties du visage (Parts of the face)</u>

548.	Hair	Cheveux (mpl)
549.	Forehead	Front (m)
550.	Temple	Tempe (f)
551.	Eyebrow	Sourcil (m)
552.	Eye	Oeil (m)
553.	Eyelid	Paupière (f)
554.	Eyelash	Cil (m)
555.	Nose	Nez (m)
556.	Nostril	Narine (f)
557.	Ear	Oreille (f)
558.	Mouth	Bouche (f)
559.	Cheek	Joue (f)
560.	Tooth	Dent (f)
561.	Tongue	Langue (f)
562.	Jaw	Mâchoire (f)
563.	Chin	Menton (m)
564.	Lip	Lèvre (f)

Monnaie (Currency)

565.	Dollar	Dollar (m)
566.	Euro	Euro (m)
567.	Pound	Livre (f)
568.	Dinar	Dinar (m)
569.	Canadian dollar	Dollar canadien (m)
570.	Rupee	Roupie (f)
571.	Yuan	Yuan (m)
572.	Riyal	Riyal (m)
573.	Yen	Yen (m)
574.	Ruble	Rouble (m)
575.	Peso	Peso (m)

<u>Directions (Directions)</u>

576.	I am lost	Je suis perdu(m) /perdue(f)
577.	I have lost…	J'ai perdu…
578.	Where is…?	Où est le/la…?
579.	Where are the toilets?	Où sont les toilettes?
580.	It's to the left	C'est à gauche
581.	It's to the right	C'est à droite
582.	It's straight ahead	C'est tout droit
583.	It's next to	C'est à côté de
584.	Which way?	Par où?
585.	Is it far?	C'est loin?
586.	Is it near?	C'est proche?

<u>Où est….?(Where is…?)</u>

587.	Where is the bus stop?	Où est l'arrêt de bus?
588.	Where is the train station?	Où est la gare?
589.	Where is the airport?	Où est l'aéroport?
590.	Where is the metro station?	Où est la station de métro?
591.	Where is the taxi stand?	Où est la station de taxi?
592.	Where is the nearest hospital?	Où est l'hôpital le plus proche?
593.	Where is a good restaurant/ café?	Où est un bon restaurant/café?
594.	Where is the nearest gas station?	Où est la station-service la plus proche?
595.	Where is the nearest police station?	Où est le poste de police le plus proche?
596.	Where is the beach?	Où est la plage?
597.	Where is the nearest bank?	Où est la banque la plus proche?

<u>À la banque (At the bank)</u>

598.	I would like to open an account	Je voudrais ouvrir un compte
599.	I would like to deposit/ withdraw money	Je voudrais déposer/ retirer de l'argent
600.	I would like to cash a cheque	Je voudrais toucher un chèque
601.	I would like to transfer money	Je voudrais virer de l'argent
602.	I would like to change money into dollars/euros…	Je voudrais changer de l'argent en dollars/euros…

Au restaurant (At the restaurant)

603.	A table for two/three	Une table pour deux/trois personnes
604.	The menu, please (Fixed price menu)	Le menu, s'il vous plaît
605.	Are you ready to order?	Vous avez choisi?
606.	I would like to order, please	Je voudrais commander s'il vous plaît
607.	I'll have…	Je vais prendre…
608.	What do you recommend?	Qu'est-ce que vous me conseillez?
609.	I'm vegetarian	Je suis végétarien (m) /végétarienne (f)
610.	I smoke	Je fume
611.	I don't smoke	Je ne fume pas
612.	Non-smoking area	Partie non-fumeurs
613.	I would like a jug of water	Je voudrais une carafe d'eau
614.	Mineral water/ Tap water	Eau minérale/ Eau du robinet

615.	I'll have a glass of wine	Je vais prendre un verre de vin
616.	I don't drink	Je ne bois pas
617.	May I have some more, please?	Encore un peu, sil vous plaît
618.	Cheers!	À la vôtre!
619.	It tastes delicious /terrible	C'est délicieux/terrible
620.	I can't eat chicken	Je ne mange pas de poulet
621.	I didn't order this	Je n'ai pas commandé ça
622.	I would like a coffee	Je voudrais un café
623.	I'm allergic to peanuts	Je suis allergique aux cacahuètes
624.	Service included/ not included	Service compris/ non compris
625.	May we have the bill, please?	L'addition, s'il vous plaît

Dans un magasin (In the shop)

626.	Can I help you?	Puis-je vous aider?
627.	I am looking for…	Je cherche…
628.	How much does it cost?	Ça coûte combien?
629.	It's expensive	C'est cher!
630.	It's cheap	C'est bon marché
631.	It's good	C'est bon
632.	Could I pay with a credit card?	Peux-je payer avec une carte de crédit?
633.	I'll pay cash	Je vais payer en espèces
634.	I would like to try it	Je voudrais l'essayer
635.	I would like to buy it	Je voudrais l'acheter
636.	At what time do you close?	À quelle heure fermez-vous?

<u>À l'hôtel (At the hotel)</u>

637.	I would like a room for three nights	Je voudrais une chambre pour trois nuits
638.	I would like a single room	Je voudrais une chambre pour une personne
639.	I would like a double room	Je voudrais une chambre double
640.	How much do I owe you?	Combien est-ce que je vous dois?
641.	What is the check-out time?	À quelle heure faut-il libérer la chambre?
642.	Could you call a taxi for me, please?	Pouvez-vous m'appeler un taxi, s'il vous plaît?

À la gare/l'aéroport...(At the train station/airport...)

643.	Where is the ticket counter?	Où est le guichet?
644.	I would like to reserve a ticket	Je voudrais réserver un billet
645.	I would like a one-way ticket for...	Je voudrais un billet en aller simple pour...
646.	I would like a return ticket for. . .	Je voudrais un billet en aller retour pour. . .
647.	I would like the schedule	Je voudrais l'horaire
648.	At what time does the next train leave?	À quelle heure part le prochain train?